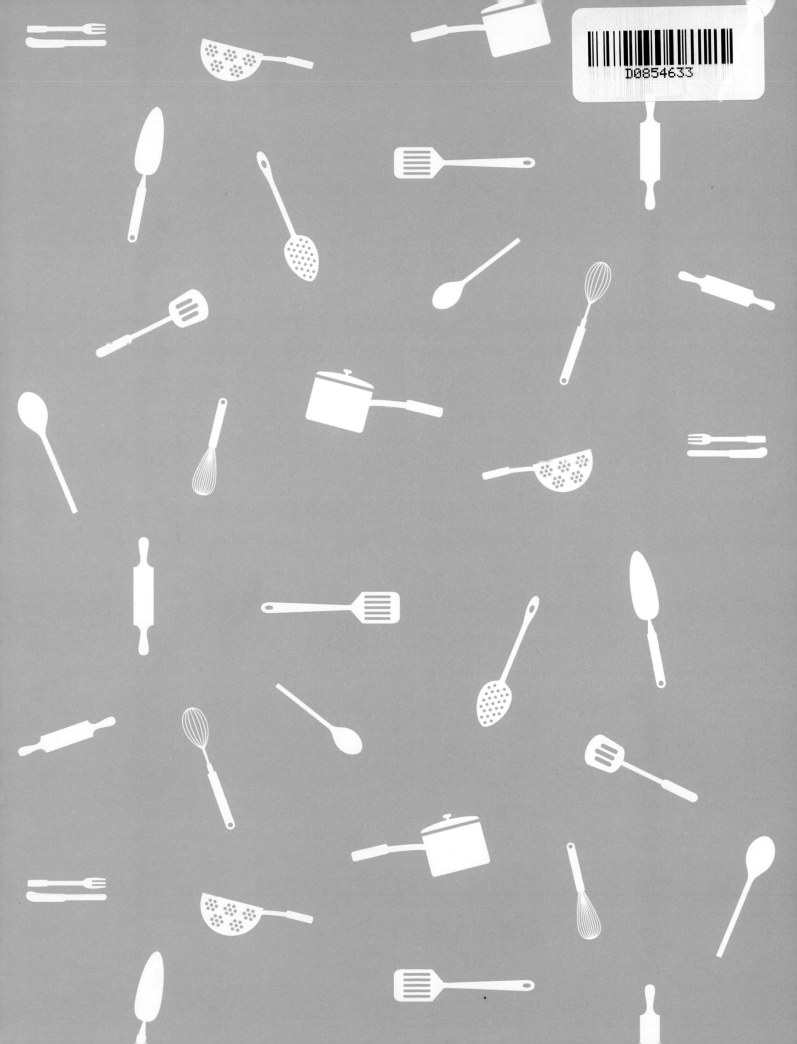

MAKE YOUR OWN
WHOOPIE PIES
& OTHER SWEET TREATS

BY DOMINIQUE GODFREY
& NANCY LAMBERT

Licensed exclusively to Top That Publishing Ltd
Tide Mill Way, Woodbridge, Suffolk, IP12 1AP, UK
www.topthatpublishing.com
Copyright © 2013 Tide Mill Media
All rights reserved
0 2 4 6 8 9 7 5 3 1
Printed and bound in China

CONTENTS

WHOOPIE PIES

SWEET TREATS

INTRODUCTION

Creating and baking whoopie pies and other sweet treats is easy and fun when you know how!

Whether it's for a special occasion such as a birthday party or sleepover, or just for you and your family to enjoy, making sweet treats is always fun! With such a wide variety of sweet treats included, you're sure to find something to suit every occasion, from an after-school snack to a midnight feast!

Whoopie pies are a delicious sweet treat that originated from the north-east of America and are best described as a mixture between a cookie and a cake sandwiched together with a scrumptious sweet filling. Easy to bake and with an endless choice of flavours and fillings, whoopie pies are the ideal treat to prepare, bake and enjoy.

This book will provide you with a selection of delicious whoopie pie and sweet treat recipes for adults and junior chefs to make together. And remember, once you have perfected the recipes, don't be afraid to experiment with the ingredients, flavours and toppings to create and decorate your very own whoopie pies and sweet treats!

COOL COOKING TIPS!

- Make sure you use the freshest ingredients available.
- You may find it easier to use special whoopie pie trays. These have shallow, round holes to make sure the whoopie pies come out looking perfect. Whoopie pie trays can be found in some supermarkets, baking shops or online. If you haven't got whoopie pie trays, pipe or spoon the mixture onto a baking tray, trying to keep the mixture as round as possible.

EQUIPMENT

- To complete the recipes in this book, you will need to use a selection of everyday cooking equipment and utensils, such as mixing bowls, saucepans, a sieve, knives, spoons, forks, a wire cooling rack and a chopping board.

- You'll need to weigh and measure the ingredients, so you'll need a measuring jug and some kitchen scales too.

- Some of the recipes tell you to use a whisk. Ask an adult to help you use an electric whisk, or you can use a balloon whisk yourself – you'll just have to work extra hard!

- To make some of the recipes in this book, you'll need to use the correct-sized tins or other special equipment. These items (and others that you may not have to hand) are listed at the start of each recipe. All of the whoopie pie recipes will require two whoopie pie trays and a piping bag.

SAFETY & HYGIENE

- Before starting any cooking, always wash your hands.

- Cover any cuts with a plaster.

- Wear an apron to protect your clothes.

ADULT SUPERVISION
IS REQUIRED FOR
ALL RECIPES

- Always make sure that all the equipment you use is clean.

- If you need to use a sharp knife to cut up something hard, ask an adult to help you. Always use a chopping board.

- Remember that trays in the oven and pans on the cooker can get very hot. Always ask an adult to turn on the oven and get things in and out of the oven for you.

- Always ask an adult for help if you are using anything electrical – like an electric whisk.

- Be careful when heating anything in a pan on top of the cooker. Keep the handle turned to one side to avoid accidentally knocking the pan.

- Keep your pets out of the kitchen while cooking.

GETTING STARTED

MEASURING

Use scales to weigh exactly how much of each ingredient you need or use a measuring jug to measure liquids.

MIXING

Use a spoon, balloon whisk or electric hand whisk to mix the ingredients together.

CREATING RECIPES

Once you've made a recipe in this book a few times, think about whether you could make your own version. This way you can start to make up your own recipes Try to think up names for the things you create!

PLEASE NOTE

The measurements given in this book are approximate. Use the same measurement conversions throughout your recipe (grams or ounces) to maintain the correct ratios. All of the recipes in this book have been created for adults to make with junior chefs and must not be attempted by an unsupervised child.

The 'Makes …' label is a guide only and will differ depending on the size of the mould or tray.

Read through each recipe to make sure you've got all the ingredients that you need before you start.

BLUEBERRY WHOOPIE PIES
WITH LIME CREAM CHEESE FILLING

MAKES 8

Extra equipment:
- food processor

Ingredients:
- 75 g (3 oz) unsalted butter, softened
- 150 g (5 oz) caster sugar
- 1 large egg, beaten
- 200 g (7 oz) blueberries
- 275 g (10 oz) plain flour
- $^3/_4$ teaspoon bicarbonate of soda
- $^1/_8$ teaspoon salt
- 145 ml (5 fl.oz) buttermilk
- 1 teaspoon vanilla extract

For the filling:
- 50 g (2 oz) unsalted butter
- 300 g (10 $^1/_2$ oz) icing sugar
- 125 g (4 $^1/_2$ oz) cream cheese
- 2 tablespoons fresh lime juice
- 1 tablespoon lime zest, finely grated

Preheat the oven to 180°C / 160°C fan oven / 350°F / gas mark 4

1 Grease the whoopie pie trays with a little butter.

2 Cream the softened butter and sugar together in a bowl until light and fluffy, then gradually add the beaten egg.

3 Ask an adult to process half of the blueberries in a food processor until they have broken down into a liquid or very small pieces. If you don't have a food processor, use an electric mixer.

4 Add to the creamed butter mixture and mix well for a few minutes.

5 Sift the flour, bicarbonate of soda and salt together in another bowl.

6 Gradually add a third of the dry ingredients to the butter mixture, followed by a third of the buttermilk. Continue adding both alternately, then add the vanilla extract. Mix well until all of the ingredients are combined to form a thick, smooth cake mixture.

7 Fill a piping bag or use a tablespoon or scoop to transfer the cake mixture evenly onto the whoopie pie trays.

8 Place the remaining blueberries onto the pies, pushing them carefully into the cake mixture.

9 Bake in the oven for 12–14 minutes, until risen and firm to the touch.

10 Cool for 5 minutes in the trays before transferring to a wire rack to cool completely.

FOR THE FILLING

1 Beat the butter and icing sugar together for a few minutes using a whisk or electric mixer until well mixed.

2 Add the cream cheese and beat together until the filling is light and fluffy.

3 Finally, add the lime juice and zest and mix well.

4 Using either a piping bag, scoop or a spoon, spread the filling evenly over one half of the whoopie pie and sandwich together with the second half.

1 Grease the whoopie pie trays with a little butter.

2 Cream the softened butter and sugar together in a bowl until light and fluffy, then gradually add the beaten egg and vanilla extract and mix well.

3 Sift in half of the flour, the ginger, cinnamon, nutmeg, bicarbonate of soda and salt, followed by half of the buttermilk and mix well. Then add the rest of the flour and continue mixing until combined to form a thick, smooth cake mixture.

4 Add the grated carrot and raisins and stir until evenly combined.

5 Fill a piping bag or use a tablespoon or scoop to transfer the cake mixture evenly onto the whoopie pie trays.

6 Bake in the oven for 12–14 minutes, until risen and firm to the touch.

7 Cool for 5 minutes in the trays before transferring to a wire rack to cool completely.

FOR THE FILLING

1 Beat the butter and icing sugar together for a few minutes using a whisk or electric mixer until well mixed.

2 Add the cream cheese and beat together until the filling is light and fluffy.

3 Using either a piping bag, scoop or a spoon, spread the filling evenly over one half of the whoopie pie and sandwich together with the second half.

MAKES 8

Ingredients:
- 75 g (3 oz) unsalted butter, softened
- 150 g (5 oz) light brown sugar
- 1 large egg, beaten
- 1 teaspoons vanilla extract
- 275 g (10 oz) plain flour
- 1 teaspoons ground ginger
- $1/2$ teaspoons ground cinnamon
- $1/8$ teaspoons ground nutmeg
- $3/4$ teaspoons bicarbonate of soda
- $1/8$ teaspoons salt
- 145 ml (5 fl.oz) buttermilk
- 100 g (3 $1/2$ oz) finely grated carrot
- 85 g (3 oz) raisins

For the filling:
- 50 g (2 oz) unsalted butter
- 300 g (10 $1/2$ oz) icing sugar
- 125 g (4 $1/2$ oz) cream cheese

Preheat the oven to 180°C / 160°C fan oven / 350°F / gas mark 4

CHOCOLATE & BANANA WHOOPIE PIES
WITH CHOCOLATE BUTTERCREAM

MAKES 8

Ingredients:
- 75 g (3 oz) unsalted butter, softened
- 150 g (5 oz) dark brown sugar
- 1 large egg, beaten
- 275 g (10 oz) plain flour
- 40 g (1 ½ oz) cocoa powder
- 2 ½ teaspoons bicarbonate of soda
- ⅛ teaspoon salt
- 180 ml (6 fl.oz) buttermilk
- 2 over-ripe bananas

For the filling:
- 600 g (1 lb 3 oz) icing sugar
- 80 g (3 oz) cocoa powder
- 200 g (7 oz) unsalted butter
- 5 tablespoons milk
- chocolate vermicelli sprinkles, to decorate

Preheat the oven to 180°C / 160°C fan oven / 350°F / gas mark 4

1 Grease the whoopie pie trays with a little butter.

2 Cream the softened butter and sugar together in a bowl until light and fluffy, then add the beaten egg.

3 Sift the flour, cocoa powder, bicarbonate of soda and salt together in another bowl.

4 Gradually add a third of the dry ingredients to the mixture, followed by a third of the buttermilk. Continue adding both alternately and mix well until all of the ingredients are combined to form a thick, smooth mixture.

5 Mash two over-ripe bananas in a bowl and add to the cake mixture, stirring well.

6 Fill a piping bag or use a tablespoon or scoop to transfer the cake mixture evenly onto the whoopie pie trays. Bake in the oven for 12–14 minutes until your pies are risen and firm to the touch.

7 Cool for 5 minutes in the trays before transferring your pies to a wire rack to cool completely.

FOR THE FILLING:

1 Mix the icing sugar, cocoa powder and butter together for a few minutes using a hand whisk or an electric mixer.

2 Slowly add the milk and continue mixing for 5 minutes until the buttercream is light and fluffy.

3 Using either a piping bag, scoop or a spoon, spread the buttercream evenly over one half of the whoopie pie and sandwich together carefully with the second half.

4 Sprinkle chocolate vermicelli around the edge of the whoopie pie to decorate.

CHOCOLATE CHIP WHOOPIE PIES
WITH VANILLA BUTTERCREAM

1 Grease the whoopie pie trays with a little butter.

2 Cream the softened butter and sugar together in a bowl until light and fluffy, then gradually add the beaten egg and vanilla extract.

3 Sift the flour, bicarbonate of soda and salt together in another bowl.

4 Gradually add a third of the dry ingredients to the mixture, followed by a third of the buttermilk. Continue adding both alternately and mix well until just before you add the last amount of dry ingredients.

5 Stir in the chocolate chips and then add the remaining flour to form a thick, smooth cake mixture.

6 Fill a piping bag or use a tablespoon to transfer the cake mixture evenly onto the whoopie pie trays.

7 Bake in the oven for 12–14 minutes until risen and firm to the touch.

8 Cool your pies for 5 minutes in the trays before transferring to a wire rack to cool completely.

FOR THE FILLING:

1 Beat the icing sugar and butter together for a few minutes using a whisk or electric mixer until well mixed.

2 Add the milk and vanilla extract and beat together until the buttercream is light and fluffy.

3 Using either a piping bag or a spoon, spread the buttercream evenly over one half of the whoopie pie and sandwich together with the second half.

MAKES 8

Ingredients:
- 75 g (3 oz) unsalted butter, softened
- 150 g (5 oz) caster sugar
- 1 large egg, beaten
- 1 teaspoon vanilla extract
- 275 g (10 oz) plain flour
- 3/4 teaspoon bicarbonate of soda
- 1/8 teaspoon salt
- 145 ml (5 fl.oz) buttermilk
- 100 g (3 1/2 oz) chocolate chips

For the filling:
- 500 g (1 lb 1 oz) icing sugar
- 160 g (5 1/2 oz) unsalted butter
- 3 tablespoons milk
- 1/2 teaspoon vanilla extract

Preheat the oven to 180°C / 160°C fan oven / 350°F / gas mark 4

CHOCOLATE ORANGE WHOOPIE PIES
WITH ORANGE BUTTERCREAM

MAKES 8

Ingredients:
- 75 g (3 oz) unsalted butter, softened
- 150 g (5 oz) dark brown sugar
- 1 large egg, beaten
- 1 tablespoon finely grated orange zest
- 4 tablespoons fresh orange juice
- 275 g (10 oz) plain flour
- 40 g (1 ½ oz) cocoa powder
- 1 ½ teaspoons bicarbonate of soda
- ⅛ teaspoon salt
- 145 ml (5 fl.oz) buttermilk

For the filling:
- 160 g (5 ½ oz) unsalted butter
- 500 g (1 lb 1 oz) icing sugar
- 3 tablespoons milk
- ½ teaspoon orange extract
- a drop of orange food colouring

Preheat the oven to 180°C / 160°C fan oven / 350°F / gas mark 4

1 Grease the whoopie pie trays with a little butter.

2 Cream the softened butter and sugar together in a bowl until light and fluffy, then gradually add the beaten egg until well mixed.

3 Add the grated zest and juice from an orange and mix well.

4 Sift the flour, cocoa powder, bicarbonate of soda and salt together into another bowl.

5 Gradually add a third of the dry ingredients to the mixture, followed by a third of the buttermilk. Continue adding both alternately, mixing well each time, until all of the ingredients are combined to form a thick, smooth cake mixture.

6 Fill a piping bag or use a tablespoon or scoop to transfer the cake mixture evenly onto the whoopie pie trays.

7 Bake in the oven for 12–14 minutes until risen and firm to the touch.

8 Cool for 5 minutes in the trays before transferring to a wire rack to cool completely.

FOR THE FILLING:

1 Beat the butter and icing sugar together for a few minutes using a whisk or electric mixer until well mixed.

2 Add the milk and orange extract, mixing well for several minutes until the buttercream is light and fluffy.

3 Finally, add a drop or two of orange food colouring and mix again until the colour is evenly combined.

4 Using either a piping bag, scoop or a spoon, spread the buttercream evenly over half of the whoopie pies and sandwich together with the second half.

CHOCOLATE & PEPPERMINT WHOOPIE PIES
WITH PEPPERMINT BUTTERCREAM

1 Grease the whoopie pie trays with a little butter.

2 Cream the softened butter and sugar together in a bowl until light and fluffy, then gradually add the beaten egg and peppermint extract until well mixed together.

3 Sift the flour, cocoa powder, bicarbonate of soda and salt together into another bowl.

4 Gradually add a third of the dry ingredients to the mixture, followed by a third of the buttermilk. Continue adding both alternately, mixing well each time, until all of the ingredients are combined to form a thick, smooth cake mixture.

5 Fill a piping bag or use a tablespoon or scoop to transfer the cake mixture evenly onto the whoopie pie trays.

6 Bake in the oven for 12–14 minutes until risen and firm to the touch.

7 Cool for 5 minutes in the trays before transferring to a wire rack to cool completely.

FOR THE FILLING:

1 Beat the butter and icing sugar together for a few minutes using a whisk or electric mixer until well mixed.

2 Gradually add the milk and the peppermint extract, mixing well for several minutes until the buttercream is light and fluffy.

3 Using either a piping bag, scoop or a spoon, spread the buttercream evenly onto half of the whoopie pies, sandwiching the remaining pies on top.

4 Roll the edges of each whoopie pie in the crushed candy canes to decorate.

MAKES 8

Ingredients:
- 75 g (3 oz) unsalted butter, softened
- 150 g (5 oz) dark brown sugar
- 1 large egg, beaten
- 1/2 teaspoon peppermint extract
- 275 g (10 oz) plain flour
- 40 g (1 1/2 oz) cocoa powder
- 1 1/2 teaspoons bicarbonate of soda
- 1/8 teaspoon salt
- 180 ml (6 fl.oz) buttermilk

For the filling:
- 160 g (5 1/2 oz) unsalted butter
- 500 g (1 lb 1 oz) icing sugar
- 2 tablespoons milk
- 1/2 teaspoon peppermint extract
- 85 g (3 oz) crushed candy canes (approx. 6 canes)

Preheat the oven to 180°C / 160°C fan oven / 350°F / gas mark 4

COCONUT WHOOPIE PIES
WITH COCONUT CREAM

Ingredients:
- 75 g (3 oz) unsalted butter, softened
- 150 g (5 oz) caster sugar
- 1 large egg, beaten
- 1 teaspoon coconut extract
- 275 g (10 oz) plain flour
- 50 g (2 oz) desiccated coconut
- ³/₄ teaspoon bicarbonate of soda
- ¹/₈ teaspoon salt
- 145 ml (5 fl.oz) coconut milk

For the filling:
- 80 g (3 oz) unsalted butter
- 250 g (9 oz) icing sugar
- 2 tablespoons coconut milk
- 2 tablespoons desiccated coconut (plus extra for decoration)

Preheat the oven to 180°C / 160°C fan oven / 350°F / gas mark 4

1 Grease the whoopie pie trays with a little butter.

2 Cream the softened butter and sugar together in a bowl until light and fluffy, then gradually add the beaten egg and coconut extract.

3 Sift the flour, desiccated coconut, bicarbonate of soda and salt together in another bowl.

4 Gradually add half of the dry sifted ingredients, followed by half of the coconut milk and then repeat until all of the ingredients are combined to form a thick, smooth cake mixture.

5 Fill a piping bag or use a tablespoon or scoop to transfer the cake mixture evenly onto the whoopie pie trays.

6 Bake in the oven for 12–14 minutes until risen and firm to the touch.

7 Cool for 5 minutes in the trays before transferring to a wire rack to cool completely.

FOR THE FILLING:

1 Beat the butter and icing sugar together for a few minutes using a hand whisk or an electric mixer until well mixed.

2 Add the coconut milk and the desiccated coconut and mix together for several minutes until the buttercream is light and fluffy.

3 Using either a piping bag, scoop or a spoon, spread the buttercream evenly over one half of the whoopie pie and sandwich together with the second half.

4 Sprinkle extra desiccated coconut around the edge of the whoopie pie to decorate.

16

1 Grease the whoopie pie trays with a little butter.

2 Cream the softened butter and sugar together in a bowl until light and fluffy, then gradually add the beaten egg and vanilla extract until well mixed.

3 Sift the flour, cocoa powder, bicarbonate of soda and salt together into another bowl.

4 Gradually add a third of the dry ingredients to the mixture, followed by a third of the buttermilk. Continue adding both alternately, mixing well each time, until all of the ingredients are combined to form a thick, smooth cake mixture.

5 Fill a piping bag or use a tablespoon or scoop to transfer the cake mixture evenly onto the whoopie pie trays.

6 Bake in the oven for 12–14 minutes until risen and firm to the touch.

7 Cool for 5 minutes in the trays before transferring to a wire rack to cool completely.

FOR THE FILLING:

1 Beat the butter, icing sugar and cocoa powder together for a few minutes using a hand whisk or an electric mixer until well mixed.

2 Gradually add the milk, mixing well for several minutes until the buttercream is light and fluffy.

3 Using either a piping bag, scoop or a spoon, spread the buttercream evenly onto half of the whoopie pies, sandwiching the remaining pies on top.

4 Carefully melt the chocolate in a microwave stirring at 30-second intervals, or melt the chocolate in a bowl over a saucepan of simmering water, making sure the bowl doesn't touch the water.

5 Carefully dip half of each whoopie pie into the melted chocolate, then place carefully on a cooling tray to set. Put baking paper underneath the tray to catch any excess dripping chocolate.

MAKES 8

Extra equipment:
- baking paper

Ingredients:
- 75 g (3 oz) unsalted butter, softened
- 150 g (5 oz) dark brown sugar
- 1 large egg, beaten
- 1 teaspoon vanilla extract
- 275 g (10 oz) plain flour
- 40 g (1 ½ oz) cocoa powder
- 1 ½ teaspoons bicarbonate of soda
- ½ teaspoon salt
- 180 ml (6 fl.oz) buttermilk

For the filling:
- 200 g (7 oz) unsalted butter
- 600 g (1 lb 3 oz) icing sugar
- 80 g (3 oz) cocoa powder
- 5 tablespoons milk
- 150 g (5 oz) dark chocolate

Preheat the oven to 180°C / 160°C fan oven / 350°F / gas mark 4

17

GINGERBREAD WHOOPIE PIES
WITH LEMON BUTTERCREAM

MAKES 8

Ingredients:
- 75 g (3 oz) unsalted butter, softened
- 150 g (5 oz) brown sugar
- 1 large egg, beaten
- 1 tablespoon black treacle
- 275 g (10 oz) plain flour
- 1 $\frac{1}{2}$ teaspoons ground ginger
- $\frac{1}{8}$ teaspoon ground cinnamon
- $\frac{1}{8}$ teaspoon ground nutmeg
- $\frac{1}{8}$ teaspoon ground cloves
- $\frac{3}{4}$ teaspoon bicarbonate of soda
- $\frac{1}{8}$ teaspoon salt
- 145 ml (5 fl.oz) buttermilk

For the filling:
- 500 g (10 $\frac{1}{2}$ oz) icing sugar
- 160 g (5 $\frac{1}{2}$ oz) unsalted butter
- 2 tablespoons milk
- 2 tablespoons fresh lemon juice
- 2 tablespoons lemon zest, finely grated

Preheat the oven to 180°C / 160°C fan oven / 350°F / gas mark 4

1 Grease the whoopie pie trays with a little butter.

2 Cream the softened butter and sugar together in a bowl until light and fluffy, then gradually add the beaten egg and black treacle and mix well.

3 Sift in half of the flour, ginger, cinnamon, nutmeg, cloves, bicarbonate of soda and salt, followed by half of the buttermilk. Repeat until all of the ingredients are combined to form a thick, smooth cake mixture.

4 Fill a piping bag or use a tablespoon or scoop to transfer the cake mixture evenly onto the whoopie pie trays.

5 Bake in the oven for 12–14 minutes until risen and firm to the touch.

6 Cool for 5 minutes in the trays before transferring to a wire rack to cool completely.

FOR THE FILLING:

1 Beat the icing sugar and butter together for a few minutes using a whisk or electric mixer until well mixed.

2 Add the milk, lemon juice and zest and mix for 5 minutes until the buttercream is light and fluffy.

3 Using either a piping bag, scoop or a spoon, spread the buttercream evenly over one half of the whoopie pie and sandwich together carefully with the second half.

1 Grease the whoopie pie trays with a little butter.

2 Cream the softened butter and sugar together in a bowl until light and fluffy, then gradually add the beaten egg, lemon juice and finely grated lemon zest.

3 Sift the flour, bicarbonate of soda and salt together in another bowl.

4 Gradually add a third of the dry ingredients to the mixture, followed by a third of the buttermilk. Continue adding both alternately and mix well until all of the ingredients are combined to form a thick, smooth cake mixture.

5 Fill a piping bag or use a tablespoon to transfer the cake mixture evenly onto the whoopie pie trays.

6 Bake in the oven for 12–14 minutes until risen and firm to the touch.

7 Cool for 5 minutes in the trays before transferring to a wire rack to cool completely.

FOR THE FILLING:

1 Beat the butter and icing sugar together for a few minutes using a whisk or electric mixer until well mixed.

2 Add the cream cheese and beat together until the filling is light and fluffy.

3 Finally, add the lemon juice and mix well.

4 Using either a piping bag or a spoon, spread the filling evenly over one half of the whoopie pie and sandwich together with the second half.

MAKES 8

Ingredients:
- 75 g (3 oz) unsalted butter, softened
- 150 g (5 oz) caster sugar
- 1 large egg, beaten
- 2 tablespoons fresh lemon juice
- 2 teaspoons lemon zest, finely grated
- 275 g (10 oz) plain flour
- $3/4$ teaspoon bicarbonate of soda
- $1/8$ teaspoon salt
- 145 ml (5 fl.oz) buttermilk

For the filling:
- 50 g (2 oz) unsalted butter
- 300 g (10 $1/2$ oz) icing sugar
- 125 g (4 $1/2$ oz) cream cheese
- 2 tablespoons fresh lemon juice

Preheat the oven to 180°C / 160°C fan oven / 350°F / gas mark 4

OATMEAL WHOOPIE PIES
WITH MAPLE BUTTERCREAM

Ingredients:
- 75 g (3 oz) unsalted butter, softened
- 150 g (5 oz) light brown sugar
- 1 large egg, beaten
- 250 g (9 oz) plain flour
- 1/2 teaspoon bicarbonate of soda
- 1/2 teaspoon baking powder
- 1/2 teaspoon ground cinnamon
- 1/8 teaspoon salt
- 65 ml (2 fl.oz) boiling water
- 90 g (3 oz) rolled oats

For the filling:
- 160 g (6 oz) unsalted butter
- 500 g (1 lb 1 oz) icing sugar
- 50 g (3 tablespoons) maple syrup
- 2 tablespoons milk
- 50 g (2 tablespoons) chopped pecan nuts

Preheat the oven to 180°C / 160°C fan oven / 350°F / gas mark 4

1 Grease the whoopie pie trays with a little butter.

2 Cream the softened butter and sugar together in a bowl until light and fluffy, then gradually add the beaten egg and mix well.

3 Sift the flour, bicarbonate of soda, baking powder, cinnamon and salt together in another bowl.

4 Gradually add the dry ingredients to the butter mixture, along with the boiling water. Mix well, then stir in the oats.

5 Fill a piping bag or use a tablespoon to transfer the cake mixture evenly onto the whoopie pie trays.

6 Bake in the oven for 12–14 minutes until risen and firm to the touch.

7 Cool for 5 minutes in the trays before transferring to a wire rack to cool completely.

FOR THE FILLING:

1 Beat the butter and icing sugar together for a few minutes using a hand whisk or an electric mixer until well mixed.

2 Add the maple syrup and milk and mix for several minutes until the buttercream is light and fluffy.

3 Using a spoon, spread the buttercream evenly over one half of the whoopie pie and sandwich together with the second half.

4 Sprinkle chopped pecan nuts around the edge of the whoopie pie to decorate.

1 Grease the whoopie pie trays with a little butter.

2 Cream the softened butter and sugar together in a bowl until light and fluffy, then gradually add the beaten egg until well mixed.

3 Melt the chocolate in the microwave, stirring at 30 second intervals, being careful not to burn it.

4 Ask an adult to process the biscuits in a food processor until they have a crumb-like consistency. If you haven't got a food processor, use an electric mixer.

5 Combine the melted chocolate with the biscuit crumbs and add, with the vanilla extract, to the cake mixture.

6 Sift the flour, bicarbonate of soda and salt together into another bowl.

7 Gradually add a third of the dry ingredients to the mixture, followed by a third of the buttermilk. Continue adding both alternately and mix well until all of the ingredients are combined to form a thick, smooth cake mix.

8 Fill a piping bag or use a tablespoon to transfer the cake mixture evenly onto the whoopie pie trays.

9 Bake in the oven for 12–14 minutes until risen and firm to the touch.

10 Cool for 5 minutes in the tray before transferring to a wire rack to cool completely.

FOR THE FILLING:

1 Beat the butter and icing sugar together for a few minutes using a hand whisk or an electric mixer until well mixed.

2 Add the milk and vanilla extract, mixing well for several minutes until the buttercream is light and fluffy.

3 Roughly chop the biscuits into small pieces and add to the buttercream.

4 Using a spoon, spread the buttercream evenly over one half of the whoopie pie and sandwich together with the second half.

Extra equipment:
• food processor

MAKES 8

Ingredients:
• 75 g (3 oz) unsalted butter, softened
• 150 g (5 oz) light brown sugar
• 1 large egg, beaten
• 100 g (3 ¹/₂ oz) dark chocolate
• 100 g (3 ¹/₂ oz) vanilla-filled (Oreo) chocolate biscuits, crumbled
• 1 teaspoon vanilla extract
• 250 g (10 oz) plain flour
• 1 ¹/₂ teaspoons bicarbonate of soda
• ¹/₈ teaspoon salt
• 145 ml (5 fl.oz) buttermilk

For the filling:
• 160 g (6 oz) unsalted butter
• 500 g (1 lb 1 oz) icing sugar
• 50 ml (1 ¹/₂ fl.oz) milk
• ¹/₂ teaspoon vanilla extract
• 100 g (3 ¹/₂ oz) vanilla-filled (Oreo) chocolate biscuits

Preheat the oven to 180°C / 160°C fan oven / 350°F / gas mark 4

21

PEANUT BUTTER WHOOPIE PIES
WITH CHOCOLATE & HAZELNUT BUTTERCREAM

MAKES 8

Ingredients:
- 75 g (3 oz) unsalted butter, softened
- 150 g (5 oz) caster sugar
- 1 large egg, beaten
- 1 teaspoon vanilla extract
- 75 g (3 oz) peanut butter
- 275 g (10 oz) plain flour
- ³/₄ teaspoon bicarbonate of soda
- ¹/₈ teaspoon salt
- 145 ml (5 fl.oz) buttermilk

For the filling:
- 110 g (4 oz) unsalted butter
- 300 g (10 ¹/₂ oz) chocolate and hazelnut spread
- 125 g (4 ¹/₂ oz) icing sugar
- 2 tablespoons milk

Preheat the oven to 180°C / 160°C fan oven / 350°F / gas mark 4

1 Grease the whoopie pie trays with a little butter.

2 Cream the softened butter and sugar together in a bowl until light and fluffy, then gradually add the beaten egg, vanilla extract and peanut butter.

3 Sift the flour, bicarbonate of soda and salt together in another bowl.

4 Gradually add a third of the dry ingredients to the mixture, followed by a third of the buttermilk. Continue adding both alternately and mix well until all of the ingredients are combined to form a thick, smooth cake mixture.

5 Fill a piping bag or use a tablespoon or scoop to transfer the cake mixture evenly onto the whoopie pie trays.

6 Bake in the oven for 12–14 minutes until risen and firm to the touch.

7 Cool for 5 minutes in the trays before transferring to a wire rack to cool completely.

FOR THE FILLING:

1 Beat the butter for a few minutes using a whisk or electric mixer until smooth.

2 Add the chocolate and hazelnut spread and mix again until combined.

3 Add the icing sugar, a little at a time, until well mixed.

4 Finally, add the milk and mix until you have a smooth consistency.

5 Using a spoon, spread the buttercream evenly over one half of the whoopie pie and sandwich together with the second half.

RAINBOW WHOOPIE PIES
WITH RAINBOW BUTTERCREAM

1 Grease the whoopie pie trays with a little butter.

2 Cream the softened butter and sugar together in a bowl until light and fluffy, then gradually add the beaten egg and vanilla extract.

3 Sift the flour, bicarbonate of soda and salt together in another bowl.

4 Gradually add a third of the dry ingredients to the mixture, followed by a third of the buttermilk. Continue adding both alternately and mix well until all of the ingredients are combined to form a thick, smooth cake mixture. Be careful not to overmix.

5 Separate equal measures of the prepared cake mixture into five bowls and add different food colourings to each bowl, mixing well.

6 Transfer the different coloured cake mixtures into piping bags (do not cut the end until the bags are filled).

7 Cut the tip of each bag and squeeze out a small amount of coloured cake mix into each pie tray compartment. Repeat this process with each colour until the tray is full.

8 Bake in the oven for 12–14 minutes until risen and firm to the touch.

9 Cool for 5 minutes in the trays before transferring to a wire rack to cool completely.

FOR THE FILLING:

1 Beat the butter and icing sugar together for a few minutes using a hand whisk or an electric mixer until well mixed.

2 Add the milk and beat together until the buttercream is light and fluffy.

3 Separate the icing into two bowls and colour with two contrasting rainbow colours.

4 Fill two small piping bags with the different coloured icing. Then snip the ends of both bags and insert them into the large piping bag.

5 Carefully pipe the icing onto one half of the rainbow whoopie, ensuring that both colours are visible. Sandwich together and enjoy!

(MAKES 8)

Extra equipment:
- 5 piping bags
- 2 small piping bags
- 1 large piping bag with a large round nozzle

Ingredients:
- 75 g (3 oz) unsalted butter, softened
- 150 g (5 oz) caster sugar
- 1 large egg, beaten
- 1 teaspoon vanilla extract
- 275 g (10 oz) plain flour
- $^3/_4$ teaspoon bicarbonate of soda
- $^1/_8$ teaspoon salt
- 145 ml (5 fl.oz) buttermilk
- 5 food colourings, any colours

For the filling:
- 80 g (3 oz) unsalted butter
- 250 g (9 oz) icing sugar
- 2 tablespoons milk
- 2 food colourings, any colours

Preheat the oven to 180°C / 160°C fan oven / 350°F / gas mark 4

RASPBERRY RIPPLE WHOOPIE PIES
WITH RASPBERRY RIPPLE CREAM CHEESE FILLING

Extra equipment:
• food processor

Ingredients:
• 75 g (3 oz) unsalted butter, softened
• 150 g (5 oz) caster sugar
• 1 large egg, beaten
• 250 g (9 oz) raspberries
• 325 g (11 ¹/₂ oz) plain flour
• ³/₄ teaspoon bicarbonate of soda
• ¹/₈ teaspoon salt
• 145 ml (5 fl.oz) buttermilk

For the filling:
• 50 g (2 oz) unsalted butter
• 300 g (10 ¹/₂ oz) icing sugar
• 125 g (4 ¹/₂ oz) cream cheese
• 125 g (4 ¹/₂ oz) raspberries
• 40 g (1 ¹/₂ oz) icing sugar, sieved
• 1 ¹/₂ teaspoons lemon juice

Preheat the oven to 180°C / 160°C fan oven / 350°F / gas mark 4

1 Grease the whoopie pie trays with a little butter.

2 Cream the softened butter and sugar together in a bowl until light and fluffy, then gradually add the beaten egg.

3 Ask an adult to process half of the raspberries in a food processor until they have broken down into a liquid. If you don't have a food processor, use a hand held mixer.

4 Add to the creamed butter mixture and mix well for a few minutes.

5 Sift the flour, bicarbonate of soda and salt together in another bowl.

6 Gradually add a third of the dry ingredients to the mixture, followed by a third of the buttermilk. Continue adding both alternately and mix well until all of the ingredients are combined to form a thick, smooth cake mixture.

7 Add the remaining whole raspberries and mix well with a spoon until evenly combined.

8 Fill a piping bag or use a tablespoon to transfer the cake mixture evenly onto the whoopie pie trays.

9 Bake in the oven for 12–14 minutes until risen and firm to the touch.

10 Cool for 5 minutes in the trays before transferring to a wire rack to cool completely.

FOR THE FILLING:

1 Beat the butter and icing sugar together for a few minutes until well mixed.

2 Add the cream cheese and beat together until the filling is light and fluffy.

3 Process the raspberries in a food processor and then add the sieved icing sugar and lemon juice.

4 Pour the raspberry sauce through a sieve into a jug, to remove all of the seeds.

5 Using a tablespoon, spread the filling onto half of the whoopie pies, drizzle with raspberry sauce and then sandwich together with the remaining halves.

RED VELVET WHOOPIE PIES
WITH MARSHMALLOW CREAM CHEESE FILLING

1 Grease the whoopie pie trays with a little butter.

2 Cream the softened butter and sugar together in a bowl until light and fluffy, then gradually add the beaten egg, vanilla extract and red food colouring, ensuring everything is well mixed.

3 Sift in half of the flour and cocoa powder to the mixture, followed by half of the buttermilk and then repeat until all of the ingredients are combined to form a thick, smooth cake mixture.

4 Add the bicarbonate of soda, white wine vinegar and salt and continue to mix well for a few minutes.

5 Fill a piping bag or use a tablespoon or scoop to transfer the cake mixture onto the whoopie pie trays.

6 Bake in the oven for 12–14 minutes until risen and firm to the touch.

7 Cool for 5 minutes in the trays before transferring to a wire rack to cool completely.

FOR THE FILLING:

1 Beat the butter and cream cheese together. Then, using a spoon dipped in hot water, add the marshmallow fluff.

2 Gradually add all of the icing sugar and continue to mix for several minutes, until you are left with a smooth, silky-looking filling.

3 Using either a piping bag, scoop or a spoon, spread the filling evenly over one half of the whoopie pie and sandwich together with the second half.

MAKES 8

Ingredients:
- 75 g (3 oz) unsalted butter, softened
- 150 g (5 oz) light brown sugar
- 1 large egg, beaten
- 1 teaspoon vanilla extract
- 1 teaspoon red food colouring
- 275 g (10 oz) plain flour
- 2 tablespoons cocoa powder
- 145 ml (5 fl.oz) buttermilk
- $^3/_4$ teaspoon bicarbonate of soda
- $^3/_4$ teaspoon white wine vinegar
- $^1/_8$ teaspoon salt

For the filling:
- 110 g (4 oz) butter
- 225 g (8 oz) cream cheese
- 1 jar (7 $^1/_2$ oz) marshmallow fluff
- 450 g (1 lb) icing sugar

Preheat the oven to 180°C / 160°C fan oven / 350°F / gas mark 4

SPICED APPLE & CINNAMON WHOOPIE PIES
WITH CINNAMON BUTTERCREAM

Ingredients:
- 75 g (3 oz) unsalted butter, softened
- 150 g (5 oz) light brown soft sugar
- 1 large egg, beaten
- 275 g (10 oz) plain flour
- $^1/_2$ teaspoon ground cinnamon
- $^1/_4$ teaspoon ground nutmeg
- $^1/_8$ teaspoon ground cloves
- $^3/_4$ teaspoon bicarbonate of soda
- $^1/_8$ teaspoon salt
- 145 ml (5 fl.oz) buttermilk
- 1 bramley apple, peeled, cored and cut into small pieces

For the filling:
- 50 g (2 oz) unsalted butter
- 300 g (10 $^1/_2$ oz) icing sugar
- $^1/_8$ teaspoon ground cinnamon
- 125 g (4 $^1/_2$ oz) cream cheese

Preheat the oven to 180°C / 160°C fan oven / 350°F / gas mark 4

1. Grease the whoopie pie trays with a little butter.

2. Cream the softened butter and sugar together in a bowl until light and fluffy, then gradually add the beaten egg.

3. Sift in half of the flour, the cinnamon, nutmeg, cloves, bicarbonate of soda and salt, followed by half of the buttermilk. Repeat until all of the ingredients are combined to form a thick, smooth cake mixture.

4. Stir in the small apple pieces.

5. Fill a piping bag or use a tablespoon to transfer the cake mixture evenly onto the whoopie pie trays.

6. Bake in the oven for 12–14 minutes until risen and firm to the touch.

7. Cool for 5 minutes in the trays before transferring to a wire rack to cool completely.

FOR THE FILLING:

1. Beat the butter, icing sugar and cinnamon together for a few minutes using a hand whisk or an electric mixer until well mixed.

2. Add the cream cheese and beat together until the buttercream is light and fluffy.

3. Using either a piping bag or a spoon, spread the buttercream evenly over one half of the whoopie pie and sandwich together with the second half.

STRAWBERRIES & CREAM WHOOPIE PIES
WITH WHIPPED CREAM & FRESH STRAWBERRY FILLING

1 Grease the whoopie pie trays with a little butter.

2 Ask an adult to add the halved strawberries to a food processor and carefully pulse for a few seconds until the strawberries have broken down into small pieces. Transfer to a bowl and set to one side. If you haven't got a food processor, use a hand held mixer.

3 Cream the softened butter and sugar together in a bowl until light and fluffy, then gradually add the beaten egg. Sift the flour, bicarbonate of soda and salt together in another bowl.

4 Gradually add a third of the dry ingredients to the mixture, followed by a third of the buttermilk. Continue adding both alternately and mix well until all of the ingredients are combined to form a thick, smooth cake mixture.

5 Fold in the chopped strawberries until they are combined evenly with the cake mixture.

6 Fill a piping bag or use a tablespoon to transfer the cake mixture evenly onto the whoopie pie trays.

7 Bake in the oven for 12–14 minutes until risen and firm to the touch.

8 Cool for 5 minutes in the trays before transferring to a wire rack to cool completely

FOR THE FILLING:

1 Whip the cream using an electric whisk or free-standing mixer until stiff peaks form.

2 Carefully spoon or pipe the cream onto a whoopie pie half.

3 Thinly slice the strawberries and lay them on top of the cream before sandwiching together with another whoopie pie half.

4 Remember to cover the whipped cream and store in the refrigerator if you are not using it straight away.

MAKES 8

Extra equipment:
- food processor

Ingredients:
- 150 g (5 oz) strawberries, hulled and halved
- 75 g (3 oz) unsalted butter, softened
- 150 g (5 oz) light brown sugar
- 1 large egg, beaten
- 275 g (10 oz) plain flour
- $3/4$ teaspoon bicarbonate of soda
- $1/8$ teaspoon salt
- 145 ml (5 fl.oz) buttermilk

For the filling:
- 275 g (9 $1/2$ oz) whipping cream
- 150 g (5 oz) fresh strawberries

Preheat the oven to 180°C / 160°C fan oven / 350°F / gas mark 4

27

VANILLA BEAN WHOOPIE PIES
WITH CHOCOLATE BUTTERCREAM

MAKES 8

Ingredients:
- 75 g (3 oz) unsalted butter, softened
- 150 g (5 oz) caster sugar
- 1 large egg, beaten
- 275 g (10 oz) plain flour
- $3/4$ teaspoon bicarbonate of soda
- $1/8$ teaspoon salt
- 145 ml (5 fl.oz) buttermilk
- 1 vanilla bean (or 1 teaspoon vanilla extract)

For the filling:
- 100 g (3 $1/2$ oz) unsalted butter, softened
- 300 g (10 $1/2$ oz) icing sugar
- 40 g (1 $1/2$ oz) cocoa powder
- 40 ml (1 $1/2$ fl.oz) whole milk

Preheat the oven to 180°C / 160°C fan oven / 350°F / gas mark 4

1 Grease the whoopie pie trays with a little butter.

2 Cream the softened butter and sugar together in a bowl until light and fluffy, then gradually add the beaten egg until well mixed.

3 Sift the flour, bicarbonate of soda and salt together into another bowl.

4 Gradually add a third of the dry ingredients to the mixture, followed by a third of the buttermilk. Continue adding both alternately and mix well until all of the ingredients are combined to form a thick, smooth cake mixture.

5 Scrape the seeds from the vanilla bean and add to the mixture. Mix for one minute. Alternatively, add 1 teaspoon of vanilla extract and mix.

6 Fill a piping bag or use a tablespoon to transfer the cake mixture evenly onto the whoopie pie trays.

7 Bake in the oven for 12–14 minutes until risen and firm to the touch.

8 Cool for 5 minutes in the trays before transferring to a wire rack to cool completely.

FOR THE FILLING:

1 Beat the butter, icing sugar and cocoa powder together for a few minutes using a hand whisk or an electric mixer until well mixed.

2 Add the milk and mix well for several minutes until the buttercream is light and fluffy.

3 Using either a piping bag or a spoon, spread the buttercream evenly over one half of the whoopie pie and sandwich together with the second half.

WHITE CHOCOLATE & MARSHMALLOW WHOOPIE PIES
WITH WHITE CHOCOLATE MARSHMALLOW FILLING

1 Grease the whoopie pie trays with a little butter.

2 Cream the softened butter and sugar together in a bowl until light and fluffy, then gradually add the beaten egg until well mixed.

3 Sift the flour, bicarbonate of soda and salt together into another bowl.

4 Gradually add a third of the dry ingredients to the mixture, followed by a third of the buttermilk. Continue adding both alternately and mix well until all of the ingredients are combined to form a thick, smooth cake mixture.

5 Add the broken pieces of white chocolate and stir until evenly combined.

6 Fill a piping bag or use a tablespoon to transfer the cake mixture evenly onto the whoopie pie trays.

7 Bake in the oven for 12–14 minutes until risen and firm to the touch.

8 Cool for 5 minutes in the trays before transferring to a wire rack to cool completely.

FOR THE FILLING:

1 Break the chocolate into small pieces and carefully melt the chocolate in a microwave, stirring at 30 second intervals. Alternatively, melt the chocolate in a bowl over a saucepan of simmering water, making sure the bowl doesn't touch the water.

2 Add the melted chocolate to the marshmallow fluff and mix well.

3 Spread the filling evenly over one half of the whoopie pie and sandwich together with the remaining halves.

MAKES 8

Ingredients:
- 75 g (3 oz) unsalted butter, softened
- 150 g (5 oz) caster sugar
- 1 large egg, beaten
- 275 g (10 oz) plain flour
- 1 1/2 teaspoons bicarbonate of soda
- 1/8 teaspoon salt
- 145 ml (5 fl.oz) buttermilk
- 100 g (3 1/2 oz) white chocolate, broken into small pieces

For the filling:
- 120 g (4 oz) white chocolate
- 210 g (7 1/2 oz) marshmallow fluff

Preheat the oven to 180°C / 160°C fan oven / 350°F / gas mark 4

SNOWBALL CUPCAKES

1 Put the cupcake cases in the cupcake tray.

2 Sift the flour into a bowl, then add the butter.

3 Use the tips of your fingers to rub the butter and flour together until the mixture becomes crumbly. Alternatively, ask an adult to use an electric whisk.

4 Add the sugar and mix it in, then stir in the eggs.

5 Finally, add the milk to make the mixture creamy, followed by the chocolate. Stir to mix.

6 Put spoonfuls of the mixture into the cupcake cases. Bake the cupcakes for 10–15 minutes, then leave them to cool on a wire rack.

7 Once cool, place the whipped cream in a piping bag and pipe onto the top of each cupcake. Finish by topping the cakes with silver balls and star sprinkles.

MAKES 12

Extra equipment:
• cupcake tray
• cupcake cases
• piping bag

Ingredients:
• 125 g (4 ¹/₂ oz) self-raising flour
• 125 g (4 ¹/₂ oz) butter, softened
• 125 g (4 ¹/₂ oz) caster sugar
• 2 large eggs
• 2–3 tablespoons milk
• 50 g (2 oz) white chocolate, broken into pieces

For the topping:
• whipped cream
• silver balls
• star sprinkles

Preheat the oven to 180°C / 160°C fan oven / 350°F / gas mark 4

1 Put the muffin cases in the muffin baking tray.

2 Ask an adult to help you grate the lemon, but be careful not to grate any of the white pith. Cut the lemon in half and squeeze the juice into a bowl and set aside.

3 Mix together the flour, baking powder, bicarbonate of soda and poppy seeds, and set aside.

4 In a large mixing bowl, cream the butter and sugar together, beating until fluffy. Beat in the eggs one at a time. Add the lemon zest and then beat in half of the dry ingredients and half of the yogurt.

5 Next, beat in the remaining dry ingredients followed by the remaining yogurt.

6 Spoon the mixture into the paper cases, and bake the muffins for 25–30 minutes, or until they are golden brown.

7 For the icing, put the icing sugar into a bowl with the lemon juice. Mix together well, until it forms a smooth paste.

8 While the muffins are still warm, spoon a little of the icing over each one. Leave to cool completely.

MAKES 12

Extra equipment:
• muffin cases
• muffin baking tray

Ingredients:
• 375 g (13 oz) plain flour
• 1 tablespoon baking powder
• $1/2$ teaspoon bicarbonate of soda
• 2 tablespoons poppy seeds
• 140 g (5 oz) unsalted butter
• 200 g (7 oz) sugar
• 2 eggs
• 1 tablespoon lemon zest
• 350 ml (12 fl.oz) plain yogurt

For the topping:
• 2 tablespoons fresh lemon juice
• 120 g (4 oz) icing sugar

Preheat the oven to 190°C / 170°C fan oven / 375°F / gas mark 5

COCONUT ICE

1 Put the tin on the greaseproof paper, and draw around it. Cut out the square so that it is large enough to overlap the sides. Then, slit the corners and put the paper into the tin.

2 Ask an adult to help you put the icing sugar, butter and sweetened condensed milk into a pan over a medium heat, and bring the mixture to the boil. Let the mixture simmer for 4 minutes, stirring all the time.

3 Remove the pan from the heat and stir in the coconut.

4 Ask an adult to pour half of the mixture into the tin. Leave it to cool and set.

5 Colour the other half of the mixture with a few drops of food colouring. Pour it on top of the mixture in the tin, and leave it to set.

6 Cut the coconut ice into slices, but be careful – it will be very crumbly!

MAKES 30

Extra equipment:
- 18 cm (7 in.) square baking tin
- greaseproof paper

Ingredients:
- 225 g (8 oz) icing sugar
- 25 g (1 oz) butter
- 150 ml (5 fl.oz) sweetened condensed milk
- 225 g (8 oz) desiccated coconut
- pink food colouring

1 Ask an adult to put a heatproof bowl over a saucepan of just-simmering water, making sure the bowl doesn't touch the water.

2 Break the plain chocolate into small pieces and put it into the bowl, and then add the cream and butter. Stir the mixture until the chocolate has melted.

3 Take the saucepan off the heat. Take the bowl off the saucepan and leave it to cool for a few minutes. Carefully pour the melted chocolate into a plastic container. Put the lid on the container and leave it in the fridge to set for 3–4 hours.

4 Remove the container from the fridge. Roll small balls of the chocolate truffle mixture in your hands.

5 Roll the balls in cocoa powder, chocolate strands or chopped nuts, and then put them into the sweet cases.

6 Store the truffles in a container in the refrigerator until you're ready to eat them or give them as a gift.

TOP TIP!
Try coating the truffles in chopped nuts or desiccated coconut

MAKES 10–15

Extra equipment:
• plastic container
• sweet cases

Ingredients:
• 150 g (6 oz) plain chocolate
• 150 ml (5 fl.oz) double cream
• 25 g (1 oz) butter

To coat the truffles any of the following:
• cocoa powder
• chocolate strands
• chopped nuts

1 Grease the baking tin with a little butter. Ask an adult to melt the butter, chocolate and golden syrup in a saucepan. When melted, mix well.

2 Put the biscuits into a freezer bag and break up with a rolling pin until you have a mixture of fine crumbs and small pieces.

3 Mix the biscuit pieces into the melted chocolate mixture in the saucepan. Then add the marshmallows, cranberries and chopped pistachios.

4 Tip into the baking tin and flatten with a spatula. Sprinkle the milk chocolate chunks over the top.

5 Refrigerate for about 2 hours, or preferably overnight.

6 To serve, cut into 25 squares. Keep refrigerated.

MAKES 25

Extra equipment:
• 23 cm (9 in.) square baking tin
• clean freezer bag
• rolling pin
• spatula

Ingredients:
• 125 g (4 1/2 oz) butter, softened
• 300 g (10 1/2 oz) dark chocolate, broken into pieces
• 45 ml (1 1/2 fl.oz) golden syrup
• 200 g (7 oz) digestive biscuits
• 100 g (3 1/2 oz) mini marshmallows
• 50 g (1 3/4 oz) dried cranberries
• 50 g (1 3/4 oz) toasted pistachios, chopped
• 50 g (1 3/4 oz) milk chocolate chunks

TOP TIP!
If you don't like marshmallows add 100 g (3 1/2 oz) raisins in step 3.

1 Line the baking tin with baking paper.

2 Ask an adult to slowly melt the dark chocolate and butter in a heavy-based saucepan.

3 Take the pan off the heat, mix in the vanilla extract and sugar and then let the mixture cool a bit.

4 In a separate bowl beat the eggs and then add to the chocolate mixture. Then, mix in the ground almonds and chopped walnuts. Pour the mixture into the baking tin and smooth the top.

5 Ask an adult to place the baking tin in the oven and bake for 25–30 minutes. The brownie should be cooked on top, but still soft underneath.

6 Once cool, remove from the tin and cut into squares.

TOP TIP! Warm brownies taste great with vanilla ice cream!

MAKES 16

Extra equipment:
- 23 cm (9 in.) square baking tin
- baking paper

Ingredients:
- 225 g (8 oz) dark chocolate
- 225 g (8 oz) butter
- 2 teaspoons vanilla extract
- 200 g (7 oz) caster sugar
- 3 eggs, beaten
- 150 g (5 1/4 oz) ground almonds
- 100 g (3 1/2 oz) walnuts, chopped

Preheat the oven to 170°C / 150°C fan oven / 340°F / gas mark 3

SWEETIE COOKIES

1. Line the baking tray with baking paper.

2. Cream the butter and sugar together in a bowl until light and fluffy.

3. Lightly beat the egg and stir into the butter mixture with the golden syrup.

4. Mix in the flour, baking powder and ground ginger. Stir until well combined.

5. Roll out the mixture until it is about 1/2 cm (1/4 in.) thick. Use the cookie cutters to cut out the cookies then place onto the baking tray. Re-roll any leftover mixture and cut again.

6. Ask an adult to place the cookies into the oven and bake for 8–10 minutes, or until golden brown.

7. Lay out on a wire rack and dust generously with icing sugar while the cookies are still warm, so the icing sugar will melt. To finish, decorate the cookies with your favourite sweets before the icing sugar sets.

MAKES 8

Extra equipment:
- baking tray
- baking paper
- rolling pin
- shaped cookie cutters

Ingredients:
- 125 g (4 oz) butter, softened
- 175 g (6 oz) caster sugar
- 1 egg
- 1 tablespoon golden syrup
- 250 g (9 oz) plain flour
- 1/2 teaspoon baking powder
- 2 teaspoons ground ginger

To decorate:
- icing sugar, for dusting
- assorted sweets

Preheat the oven to 180°C / 160°C fan oven / 350°F / gas mark 4

1. Line both baking trays with baking paper.

2. Pour the egg whites into a large, clean glass mixing bowl. Ask an adult to beat them with an electric whisk until the mixture holds stiff peaks. Alternatively, use a hand whisk — you'll just have to work extra hard!

3. Continue whisking then gradually add the caster sugar, a dessertspoonful at a time. Continue beating and adding the caster sugar. When ready, the mixture should be thick and glossy.

4. Sift a third of the icing sugar into the mixture, then gently fold it in using a large metal spoon.

5. Continue to sift and fold in the icing sugar a third at a time. Add a few drops of food colouring, if desired. Be careful not to over-mix the meringue.

6. Place the mixture into a piping bag and squeeze 3.5 cm (1 1/2 in.) 'blobs' of the mixture onto the baking trays and ask an adult to quickly place them into the oven for 1 1/4 hours, until the meringues sound crisp when tapped underneath.

7. Remove from the baking trays and leave to cool on a wire rack.

MAKES 30-40

Extra equipment:
• 2 baking trays
• baking paper
• large glass mixing bowl
• electric whisk
• sieve
• large metal spoon
• piping bag

Ingredients:
• 4 large eggs, whites only
• 115 g (4 oz) caster sugar
• 115 g (4 oz) icing sugar
• food colouring (optional)

Preheat the oven to 110°C / 90°C fan oven / 230°F / gas mark 1/4

CHOCOLATE FONDANT FANCIES

Extra equipment:
- 23 cm (9 in.) square baking tin
- baking paper
- whisk

Ingredients:
- 175 g (6 oz) unsalted butter, plus extra for greasing
- 150 g (5 ½ oz) caster sugar
- 3 eggs
- 175 g (6 oz) plain flour
- 1 teaspoon baking powder

For the icing:
- 25 g (1 oz) unsalted butter
- 90 g (3 oz) icing sugar, sifted
- 50 g (1 ¾ oz) dark chocolate
- 50 g (1 ¾ oz) white chocolate
- 100 ml (3 ½ fl.oz) boiling water
- 75 g (2 ½ oz) mascarpone
- red writing icing, to decorate

Preheat the oven to 140°C / 120°C fan oven / 280°F / gas mark 1

1 Whisk the butter and sugar together in a large bowl until pale and fluffy. Gradually add the eggs, whisking continuously. Then, carefully mix in the flour and baking powder until well combined.

2 Spoon the cake batter into the baking tin and bake for 25–30 minutes, until risen and golden. Set aside to cool, then cut into squares.

TOP TIP!
Use different coloured writing icing to decorate each fondant fancy uniquely!

FOR THE ICING:

1 Put a heatproof bowl over a pan of simmering water, making sure the bowl doesn't touch the water. In one bowl, mix 15 g (½ oz) butter, 45 g (1 ½ oz) icing sugar and the dark chocolate and stir until glossy and smooth. Gradually add some boiling water until the mixture is loose and slightly runny. Repeat in a separate bowl using the white chocolate and remaining butter and icing sugar.

2 Decorate each cake square with a teaspoon of mascarpone and smooth over the top. Then, spoon over enough of the dark icing to cover half of the cake squares. Repeat with the white icing. Set aside for 20–30 minutes, or until the icing has set.

3 Once cool, carefully drizzle some red writing icing over the iced fondant fancies.

1 Use a paper towel to grease the baking tray with a little butter.

2 Put the butter and both sugars in a large bowl and mix them together with a wooden spoon until they are pale, light and fluffy.

3 Add the egg and the vanilla extract and beat well.

4 Sift the flour and baking powder into the bowl. Stir them into the mixture and then add the chocolate chips.

5 Put 8–10 teaspoons of the mixture onto the baking tray – you will probably have enough mixture for two batches. Leave enough room between the cookies for them to expand while cooking. Bake the cookies for 15–20 minutes, or until golden brown.

6 Leave the cookies to cool for 2–3 minutes before lifting them onto a wire rack to cool completely.

7 Once the cookies are cool, take a scoop of ice cream and place it on top of a cookie, then sandwich another cookie on top. Eat immediately.

MAKES 8-10

Extra equipment:
• baking tray
• sieve
• ice cream scoop (optional)

Ingredients:
• 125 g (4 ½ oz) butter
• 100 g (4 oz) caster sugar
• 75 g (3 oz) brown sugar
• 1 egg
• a few drops of vanilla extract
• 150 g (5 oz) plain flour
• ½ teaspoon baking powder
• 50 g (2 oz) chocolate chips
• vanilla ice cream

Preheat the oven to 180°C / 160°C fan oven / 350°F / gas mark 4

CARAMEL SHORTCAKE

1 Grease the tin with a little butter.

2 Place the flour, caster sugar, butter and semolina into a bowl and mix together until it forms a smooth dough.

3 Press the mixture into the base of the Swiss roll tin, pushing it into all of the corners. Prick the dough with a fork and then bake in the oven for about 30–40 minutes until golden and firm. Leave to cool.

4 For the topping, ask an adult to put the butter, caster sugar, syrup and condensed milk into a saucepan and stir over a low heat until the butter has melted.

5 Stir the bubbling mixture for 5–8 minutes, stirring all of the time, until the mixture thickens.

6 Pour the mixture over the cooled shortbread and spread evenly over the base. Leave to cool.

7 Ask an adult to melt the chocolate in a heatproof bowl over a pan of simmering water, making sure the bowl doesn't touch the water. Pour the melted chocolate over the caramel mixture and then leave to cool.

8 Once cool, remove from the tin and cut into pieces.

MAKES 12

Extra equipment:
• 20 x 33 cm (8 x 13 in.) Swiss roll tin

Ingredients:
• 225 g (8 oz) plain flour
• 100 g (3 1/2 oz) caster sugar
• 225 g (8 oz) butter, softened
• 100 g (3 1/2 oz) semolina

For the topping:
• 175 g (6 oz) butter
• 175 g (6 oz) caster sugar
• 4 tablespoons golden syrup
• 400 g (14 oz) sweetened condensed milk
• 200 g (7 oz) plain chocolate, broken into pieces

Preheat the oven to 160°C / 140°C fan oven / 320°F / gas mark 2

1 Put the muffin cases into the muffin baking tray.

2 In a large bowl mix together the prune purée, brown sugar, golden syrup, pumpkin and egg whites. Stir with a wooden spoon until they are well mixed.

3 In another bowl, mix together the flour, polenta, cinnamon, nutmeg and bicarbonate of soda.

4 Add the wet ingredients to the flour mixture. Use a tablespoon to gently mix the ingredients together.

5 Use a teaspoon to divide the mixture equally into the muffin cases. Bake the muffins for 20–25 minutes, or until golden brown.

6 Place the muffins onto a wire rack to cool and then enjoy.

TOP TIP!
These pumpkin muffins are a great way to use up pumpkin flesh at Halloween.

MAKES 12

Extra equipment:
• muffin cases
• muffin baking tray

Ingredients:
• 120 g (4 oz) prunes, puréed
• 165 g (6 oz) brown sugar
• 100 g (4 oz) golden syrup
• 245 g (9 oz) pumpkin flesh, puréed
• 2 egg whites
• 170 g (6 oz) plain flour
• 50 g (2 oz) polenta
• 1 teaspoon cinnamon
• 1 teaspoon nutmeg
• 1 teaspoon bicarbonate of soda

Preheat the oven to 200°C / 180°C fan oven / 400°F / gas mark 6

FRUITY LOLLIES

1 Ask an adult to carefully cut up the pineapple into small chunks. Then, cut up the bananas into slices.

2 Place the pineapple, banana, honey and yogurt into a blender and blend until smooth. If you have not got a blender, place the ingredients into a bowl and ask an adult to blend the mixture with a hand-held electric whisk.

3 Pour the mixture into the ice lolly moulds and place in the freezer. Leave them to set for at least 4 hours, until solid.

4 Remove the ice lollies from the freezer and let them stand at room temperature for 5 minutes. Then, remove from the moulds and enjoy!

TOP TIP!
Any leftover mixture can be made into a smoothie. Just blitz it in a blender with some more yogurt and milk if it's too thick.

MAKES 6

Extra equipment:
• blender
• ice lolly moulds

Ingredients:
• 220 g (7 ¾ oz) pineapple
• 2 very ripe bananas
• 2 tablespoons clear honey
• 500 ml (16 fl.oz) plain yogurt

1 Put the muffin cases into the muffin baking tray.

2 Mash the bananas in a mixing bowl.

3 Add the caster sugar, brown sugar and eggs and stir together until well mixed.

4 Add the melted butter and mix. Sift in the bicarbonate of soda and plain flour, and then add the wholemeal flour, mixing well.

5 Add the buttermilk and walnuts. Stir the mixture until well combined.

6 Use a teaspoon to divide the mixture equally into the muffin cases. Bake the muffins for 20 minutes, or until golden brown.

7 Leave the muffins to cool on a wire rack and then enjoy.

TOP TIP!
These muffins make a deliciously different Sunday morning breakfast!

MAKES 12

Extra equipment:
• muffin cases
• muffin baking tray

Ingredients:
• 3 ripe bananas
• 100 g (4 oz) caster sugar
• 70 g (2 oz) brown sugar
• 2 eggs
• 100 g (4 oz) butter, melted
• 1 1/2 teaspoons bicarbonate of soda
• 110 g (4 oz) plain flour
• 110 g (4 oz) wholemeal flour
• 45 ml (1 1/2 fl.oz) buttermilk
• 145 g (5 oz) walnuts, chopped

Preheat the oven to 160°C / 140°C fan oven / 350°F / gas mark 4

BLUEBERRY MUFFINS

1. Place the muffin cases into the muffin baking tray.

2. Place the butter, eggs and sugar into a large bowl and beat until well mixed.

3. Mix the flour with the baking powder and sift into the butter mixture, alternating with the milk.

4. Mix in the vanilla essence, then add the blueberries. Stir everything together until just moistened.

5. Use a teaspoon to divide the mixture equally into the paper cases. Bake the muffins for 30 minutes, or until golden brown.

6. Once cooked, ask an adult to remove the muffins from the oven and cool on a wire rack.

FOR THE ICING:

1. Place the icing sugar into a bowl with the water. Mix together to form a smooth icing.

2. While the muffins are still warm, spoon a little of the icing over each one. Leave to cool completely.

MAKES 12

Extra equipment:
• muffin cases
• muffin baking tray

Ingredients:
• 55 g (2 oz) butter
• 2 eggs
• 200 g (7 oz) sugar
• 250 g (9 oz) plain flour
• 2 teaspoons baking powder
• 110 ml (4 fl.oz) milk
• 1 teaspoon vanilla essence
• 290 g (10 oz) blueberries

For the topping:
• 120 g (4 oz) icing sugar
• 1–2 tablespoons water

Preheat the oven to 160°C / 140°C fan oven / 350°F / gas mark 4

1. Grease the cake tin with a little butter.

2. Beat together the sugar and eggs until pale and fluffy. Beat in the melted butter a little at a time, making sure it is well mixed.

3. Using a metal spoon, carefully fold in the flour. Then, add the chopped white chocolate and pecan nuts, carefully mixing in a little at a time.

4. Spoon the blondie mix into the cake tin and smooth out the top.

5. Ask an adult to place in the oven and bake for 30–35 minutes, or until a skewer inserted into the centre comes out clean.

6. Leave to cool completely. Once cool, remove from the tin and cut into squares.

TOP TIP!
Try icing the blondies with vanilla buttercream mixed with some peanut butter.

MAKES 16

Extra equipment:
• 20 cm (8 in.) square cake tin

Ingredients:
• 225 g (8 oz) caster sugar
• 4 eggs
• 225 g (8 oz) butter, melted
• 150 g (5 1/2 oz) plain flour, sieved
• 225 g (8 oz) white chocolate, chopped
• 100 g (3 1/2 oz) pecan nuts, chopped

Preheat the oven to 160°C / 140°C fan oven / 350°F / gas mark 4

SCOTCH PANCAKES

1 Put the flour and bicarbonate of soda into a bowl.

2 In a separate bowl, mix the egg, oil and golden syrup and whisk together. Add the milk and mix well.

3 Pour the milk mixture into the dry ingredients and whisk thoroughly to form a batter.

4 Ask an adult to heat a non-stick frying pan. Pour in 1 1/2 tablespoons of the batter for each pancake.

5 When bubbles appear in the batter of the pancake, flip it over and cook until golden brown on both sides.

6 Cook the remaining batter and then serve warm, topped with fresh fruit and more golden syrup!

TOP TIP!
To keep pancakes warm, place them in the oven at the lowest temperature with a ramekin filled with water below to keep them moist.

MAKES 8

Extra equipment:
• whisk

Ingredients:
• 110 g (4 oz) plain flour
• 1/2 teaspoon bicarbonate of soda
• 1 egg
• 1 tablespoon vegetable oil
• 1 tablespoon golden syrup
• 150 ml (5 fl.oz) milk

To serve:
• fresh fruit (optional)
• golden syrup (optional)

1 Line the baking tray with baking paper.

2 Cream the butter and sugar together in a bowl until light and fluffy. Add the egg and vanilla extract, a little at a time, and mix well.

3 Sift the flour into the creamed mixture and, using your hands, create a smooth, firm dough. Refrigerate the mixture for 15 minutes.

4 Roll the dough out on a floured surface until it is 1 cm (1/2 in.) thick. Using the cookie cutter, cut the dough into circles and transfer to the baking tray.

5 Bake the biscuits in the oven for 8–10 minutes, or until golden brown, and then transfer to a wire rack to cool.

TOP TIP! Use other colours to make a whole swarm of bees, butterflies and bugs!

FOR THE ICING:

1 Sift the icing sugar into a bowl and add enough water to make a smooth, thick paste. Add one or two drops of red food colouring to three-quarters of the icing, reserving some white for later. With the palette knife, spread the red icing over each biscuit and leave to set.

2 Use the melted dark chocolate to decorate each biscuit with spots and a head and leave to set. To finish, use the reserved white icing for the eyes, topping them off with chocolate for the pupils.

MAKES 24

Extra equipment:
- baking tray
- baking paper
- sieve
- rolling pin
- round cookie cutter
- palette knife

Ingredients:
- 100 g (4 oz) butter
- 100 g (4 oz) caster sugar
- 1 egg
- 1 teaspoon vanilla extract
- 275 g (10 oz) plain flour

For the icing:
- 400 g (14 oz) icing sugar
- 3–4 tablespoons water
- red food colouring
- dark chocolate, melted

Preheat the oven to 190°C / 170°C fan oven / 375°F / gas mark 5

1. Cream the butter and sugar together in a large bowl, until pale and fluffy.

2. Sift in both flours and the salt and mix well.

3. Use your hands to bring the mixture together and press it into the cake tin.

4. Smooth the top with the back of a spoon. Score the mixture into eight pieces with a knife and prick each piece with a fork. Use your thumb to indent around the edge of the shortbread.

5. Put the mixture in the refrigerator for 30 minutes to firm.

6. Remove the shortbread from the refrigerator and bake for 30–35 minutes, or until pale golden brown.

7. Ask an adult to remove the shortbread from the oven and sprinkle with a little caster sugar.

8. Leave the shortbread to cool in the tin for a few minutes. Then, remove it from the tin and leave to cool completely on a wire rack.

9. Cut the shortbread into eight pieces, along the scored lines, and enjoy!

MAKES 8

Extra equipment:
• sieve
• 20 cm (8 in.) loose-bottomed round cake tin

Ingredients:
• 130 g (4 1/2 oz) butter, softened
• 60 g (2 1/2 oz) caster sugar, plus extra for sprinkling
• 130 g (4 1/2 oz) plain flour
• 60 g (2 1/2 oz) rice flour
• pinch of salt

Preheat the oven to 170°C / 150°C fan oven / 325°F / gas mark 3

1. In a large saucepan, ask an adult to melt the butter over a low heat.

2. Add the vanilla extract, and then melt the marshmallows into the butter, stirring continuously.

3. When the marshmallows have melted, add the cereal and mix until it is evenly coated.

4. Allow the mixture to cool slightly, then spoon the mixture into paper cases.

5. Leave the crispy cakes for 2–3 hours to set completely and then enjoy!

TOP TIP!
Why not add sweets or chocolate chips along with the crisped cereal!

MAKES 12

Extra equipment:
• paper cases

Ingredients:
• 50 g (2 oz) butter
• 1 teaspoon vanilla extract
• 200 g (7 oz) marshmallows
• 100 g (4 oz) crisped rice cereal

SCONES

1 Grease the baking tray with a little butter.

2 Sift together the flour, baking powder and salt into a bowl. Stir in the sugar.

3 Add the butter and rub it into the flour mixture until it resembles fine breadcrumbs.

4 Add the milk, a little at a time, until it becomes a smooth dough.

5 Lightly flour the work surface and then roll out the dough until it is about 2 cm (3/4 in.) thick.

6 Use the pastry cutter to cut the dough into round scones. Re-roll any dough that is left over and cut out more scones. Place onto the baking tray.

7 Brush the tops of the scones with the beaten egg. Ask an adult to place in the oven and bake for 10–12 minutes, or until golden brown.

8 Serve with clotted cream and jam.

MAKES 8-10

Extra equipment:
• baking tray
• sieve
• rolling pin
• 5 cm (2 in.) round pastry cutter

Ingredients:
• 225 g (8 oz) self-raising flour
• 1 teaspoon baking powder
• pinch of salt
• 25 g (1 oz) caster sugar
• 50 g (2 oz) unsalted butter, softened
• 150 ml (5 fl.oz) milk
• 1 egg, beaten
• clotted cream, to serve
• jam, to serve

Preheat the oven to 220°C / 200°C fan oven / 425°F / gas mark 7

1 Place the muffin cases in the muffin baking tray.

2 Mix together the flour, baking powder, bicarbonate of soda, sugar, cinnamon and orange zest.

3 In a separate bowl, mix the milk, egg and melted butter. Add to the flour mixture and fold together until just mixed.

4 Then, stir in the chopped dates, reserving a few to top each muffin.

5 Divide the mixture into the paper cases and place some of the reserved chopped dates on top.

6 Ask an adult to place the muffins in the oven and cook for 15–20 minutes, or until just risen and firm. Transfer to a wire rack to cool.

TOP TIP!
Why not add your favourite seeds or nuts in step 4?

MAKES 12

Extra equipment:
• muffin cases
• muffin baking tray

Ingredients:
• 225 g (8 oz) plain flour
• 1 tablespoon baking powder
• 1/2 teaspoon bicarbonate of soda
• 75 g (2 1/2 oz) demerara sugar
• 1 teaspoon cinnamon
• zest of 1 small orange
• 150 ml (5 fl oz) milk
• 1 egg
• 50 g (1 3/4 oz) butter, melted
• 250 g (9 oz) pitted dates, chopped

Preheat the oven to 200°C / 180°C fan oven / 400°F / gas mark 6

CHOCOLATE ICE CREAM

Extra equipment:
- electric whisk
- ice cream maker (optional)

Ingredients:
- 300 g (10 oz) dark chocolate, finely chopped
- 240 ml (8 fl.oz) milk
- 240 ml (8 fl.oz) double cream
- 175 g (6 oz) caster sugar
- 4 large egg yolks
- 150 ml (5 fl.oz) water

1 First, tip 200 g (7 oz) of dark chocolate into a heatproof bowl, reserving the rest to add to the ice cream later. Heat the milk, double cream and 25 g (1 oz) of caster sugar in a saucepan, then pour over the chocolate and stir until dissolved. Leave on one side until cool.

2 Ask an adult to whisk the egg yolks with an electric whisk and add this to the cooled chocolate cream mixture.

3 Next, place 150 g (5 oz) of sugar in a saucepan and add 150 ml (5 fl.oz) of water. Dissolve the sugar over a medium heat, stirring occasionally. Then, bring to a boil and cook for 5 minutes.

4 Ask an adult to pour the hot sugar syrup into the chocolate cream mixture, in a thin steady stream, whilst you whisk. Continue whisking until the mixture has thickened and is similar to a mousse – this should take about 5 minutes.

5 Add the extra chocolate and stir to blend everything together. Pour into an ice cream maker and churn until frozen. Alternatively, you could freeze the mixture in a tub, stirring it every hour to break up any ice and ensure that the chocolate is evenly mixed in.

6 Once it is frozen, scoop and serve!

1 Place the muffin cases into the muffin baking tray.

2 In a large bowl mix together the butter and sugar until the mixture is creamy.

3 Add in the eggs and beat until smooth. Blend in the cinnamon, allspice, baking powder and bicarbonate of soda.

4 Add the apple sauce and sift in the flour. Stir until just blended together.

5 Use a teaspoon to divide the mixture equally into the paper cases in the muffin tray. Place the muffins in the oven and bake for 20 minutes, or until a skewer inserted comes out clean. Leave to cool on a wire rack.

6 Mix the icing sugar and water together until they form a smooth paste. Spoon a little icing over each muffin.

7 Top with a few nuts to decorate.

TOP TIP! Make sure the muffins are completely cold before icing.

MAKES 12

Extra equipment:
• muffin cases
• muffin baking tray

Ingredients:
• 110 g (4 oz) butter
• 135 g (5 oz) sugar
• 2 eggs
• 1/2 teaspoon ground cinnamon
• 1/2 teaspoon ground allspice
• 2 teaspoons baking powder
• 1/2 teaspoon bicarbonate of soda
• 235 ml (8 fl.oz) apple sauce
• 190 g (7 oz) plain flour

For the topping:
• 120 g (4 oz) icing sugar
• 2 tablespoons water
• nuts of your choice

Preheat the oven to 180°C / 160°C fan oven / 350°F / gas mark 4

1 Sift the flour into a bowl, followed by the butter. Use the tips of your fingers to rub the butter and flour together until the mixture becomes crumbly. Alternatively, ask an adult to use an electric whisk.

2 Add the sugar and mix it in, then stir in the eggs. Finally. add the vanilla extract and milk to make the mixture creamy.

3 Put spoonfuls of the mixture into the cupcake cases. Bake the cupcakes for 10–15 minutes, until they are golden brown, then leave them to cool on a wire rack.

4 Once cool, place the whipped cream into a piping bag and pipe onto the top of the cupcakes.

5 Finish with sugar sprinkles.

TOP TIP! Instead of whipped cream, top with coloured or flavoured buttercream.

MAKES 12

Extra equipment:
• cupcake tray
• cupcake cases
• piping bag with star nozzle
Ingredients:
• 125 g (4 1/2 oz) self-raising flour
• 125 g (4 1/2 oz) butter, softened
• 125 g (4 1/2 oz) caster sugar
• 2 large eggs
• a few drops of vanilla extract
• 2–3 tablespoons milk
For the topping:
• whipped cream
• sugar sprinkles

Preheat the oven to 180°C / 160°C fan oven / 350°F / gas mark 4

1 Put the muffin cases in the muffin tray.

2 Sift the flour, sugar and baking powder into a bowl, and mix them together.

3 Pour in the egg, milk and vegetable oil and mix until all the flour is combined.

4 Fold in the cranberries, orange peel and nuts until distributed evenly throughout the mixture.

5 Use a teaspoon to transfer equal amounts of the mixture to the paper cases. Bake the muffins for 20 minutes or until they are well risen and golden brown.

6 Leave them to cool on a wire rack.

TOP TIP!
Try other berries – use raspberries or blackberries in place of the cranberries.

MAKES 12

Extra equipment:
• muffin cases
• muffin tray

Ingredients:
• 250 g (9 oz) plain flour
• 150 g (5 oz) sugar
• 1 tablespoon baking powder
• 1 egg
• 175 ml (6 fl.oz) milk
• 3 tablespoons vegetable oil
• 80 g (1 oz) chopped cranberries
• 2 tablespoons grated orange peel
• 2 tablespoons chopped pecans or walnuts

Preheat the oven to 190°C / 170°C fan oven / 375°F / gas mark 5

DATE SQUARES

1 To make the date filling, place the dates and water in a saucepan and ask an adult to cook them over a low heat, stirring occasionally, until the dates are soft and have absorbed most of the water (about 5–10 minutes). Remove from the heat and stir in the vanilla extract. Leave to cool and then place in the food processor and purée until soft. Set aside.

2 Butter the baking tin and line the bottom with baking paper.

3 To make the oaty crust, place the oats, flour, sugar, baking soda, salt and ground cinnamon into a bowl and mix well.

4 Then add the butter and combine until the mixture is crumbly. Press two thirds of the mixture into the base of the prepared tin.

5 Spread the date mixture evenly over the oaty crust and then sprinkle the remaining oat mixture evenly over the top of the dates. Bake for about 30–40 minutes or until golden brown. Place on a wire rack to cool.

6 Once it has cooled, cover the tin with cling film, and place in the refrigerator for at least one hour or until firm enough to cut easily into squares.

MAKES 20

Extra equipment:
• food processor
• 20 x 28 cm (8 x 11 in) baking tin
• baking paper
• cling film

Ingredients:
• 400 g (14 oz) pitted dried dates
• 240 ml (8 fl.oz) water
• 1 teaspoon pure vanilla extract
• 200 g (7 oz) rolled oats
• 130 g (4 1/2 oz) plain flour
• 160 g (5 1/2 oz) light brown sugar
• 1/2 teaspoon baking soda
• 1/2 teaspoon salt
• 1/8 teaspoon ground cinnamon
• 225 g (8 oz) butter, cut into pieces

Preheat the oven to 180°C / 160°C fan oven / 350°F / gas mark 4

1 Put the butter and sugar into a mixing bowl. Use a wooden spoon to beat them together until the mixture is fluffy and very pale in colour. Beat in the eggs, one at a time, adding a tablespoon of flour with each one. Sift the rest of the flour into the bowl. Use a tablespoon to mix the ingredients gently. This will make sure your mixture stays nice and fluffy.

2 Use a teaspoon to transfer equal amounts of the mixture to the cupcake cases. Bake the buns for 20–25 minutes or until they are well risen and golden brown. Leave them to cool on a wire rack.

3 To make the butterfly wings, cut a slice from the top of each cake. Now cut each slice in half.

TOP TIP!
Make sure the buns are completely cold before cutting the butterfly wings.

FOR THE TOPPING:

1 Use a wooden spoon or an electric mixer to beat the butter in a large bowl until it is soft. Sift half of the icing sugar into the bowl, and then beat it with the butter until the mixture is smooth. Then, sift the rest of the icing sugar into the bowl and add one tablespoon of milk. Beat the mixture until it is smooth and creamy.

2 Place a little buttercream icing on top of each bun. Now, gently push two of the halved slices into the icing on each bun at an angle to form pretty butterfly wings. Dust with icing sugar to finish.

MAKES 12

Extra equipment:
• cupcake cases
• cupcake tray
Ingredients:
• 100 g (4 oz) butter
• 100 g (4 oz) caster sugar
• 2 eggs
• 100 g (4 oz) self-raising flour
For the topping:
• 80 g (3 oz) butter
• 150 g (5 oz) icing sugar
• 1–2 tablespoons milk
• icing sugar, to decorate

Preheat the oven to 190°C / 170°C fan oven / 350°F / gas mark 4

CHOCOLATE CAKE

SERVES 12–14

Extra equipment:
- 20 cm (7 3/4 in) round cake tin
- greaseproof paper
- palette knife

Ingredients:
- 200 g (7 oz) dark chocolate
- 200 g (7 oz) butter, cut in pieces
- 1 tablespoon instant coffee granules
- 85 g (3 oz) self-raising flour
- 85 g (3 oz) plain flour
- ¼ teaspoon bicarbonate of soda
- 200 g (7 oz) light muscovado sugar
- 200 g (7 oz) golden caster sugar
- 25 g (1 oz) cocoa powder
- 3 eggs
- 75 ml (2 ½ fl.oz) buttermilk

For the topping:
- 200 g (7 oz) dark chocolate
- 284 ml (9 ½ fl.oz) double cream
- 2 tablespoons golden caster sugar

Preheat the oven to 160°C / 140°C fan oven / 320°F / gas mark 3

1 Butter the cake tin and line the base with greaseproof paper. Break the chocolate in pieces into a saucepan. Tip in the butter, then mix the coffee granules into 125 ml (4 fl.oz) of cold water and pour into the pan. Ask an adult to warm through over a low heat until everything has just melted.

2 While the chocolate is melting, mix the self-raising and plain flour, bicarbonate of soda, the two sugars and cocoa powder in a bowl, mixing with your hands to get rid of any lumps. Beat the eggs in a separate bowl and stir in the buttermilk.

3 Next, pour the melted chocolate mixture and the egg mixture into the flour mixture, stirring until everything is mixed to a smooth consistency. Pour this into the tin and bake for 1½ hours. Leave to cool in the tin, then turn out onto a wire rack to cool completely. Then, ask an adult to cut it into two.

FOR THE TOPPING:

1 Chop the chocolate into small pieces and tip into a bowl. Pour the cream into a pan, add the sugar, and ask an adult to heat until it is about to boil. Take off the heat and pour it over the chocolate. Stir until the chocolate has melted and the mixture is smooth.

2 Sandwich the cake layers together with just a little of the topping. Pour the rest over the cake, smoothing to cover with a palette knife.

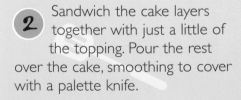

1 Ask an adult to purée the strawberries in a blender (reserving a couple for decoration), then sieve to remove any bits.

2 Put the caster sugar and egg yolks together in a bowl and whisk until thick.

3 Bring the cream to the boil in a saucepan and then gradually whisk it into the egg yolk mixture.

4 Pour the cream / egg yolk mixture back into the pan and cook over a low heat for 5 minutes, or until the mixture sticks to the back of a wooden spoon.

5 Strain the mixture into a bowl and add the strawberry purée.

6 Pour the mixture into an ice cream maker and churn until frozen. Alternatively, if you don't have an ice cream maker you can freeze your ice cream in a plastic tub in the freezer. You will need to stir the mixture every hour to break up any ice.

7 Serve your ice cream when it's frozen. Add wafer sticks to decorate!

TOP TIP!
For an extra treat, try this ice cream with the shortbread on page 48.

SERVES 6

Extra equipment:
• blender
• sieve
• ice cream maker (optional)

Ingredients:
• 350 g (12 oz) strawberries, hulled and roughly chopped
• 100 g (4 oz) caster sugar
• 2 egg yolks
• 300 ml (10 fl.oz) double cream
• wafer stick, to decorate

DICE CAKE POPS

Extra equipment:
- baking tray
- baking paper
- lollipop sticks
- polystyrene block

Ingredients:
- 500 g (18 oz) plain vanilla sponge
- 450 g (15 oz) plain white cake icing
- 400 g (14 oz) white candy coating
- 1–2 tablespoons vegetable oil
- black sugarpaste
- edible glue

1 Line the baking tray with baking paper. Break the cake into small crumbs using your fingers.

2 Add the icing into the crumbled cake mixture. Mix with your hands until you are left with a mixture that can be easily moulded.

3 Weigh out 25 g (1 oz) portions of cake mixture and mould into a cube shape.

4 Place the pops into the freezer for 10 minutes to harden before decorating.

5 Place the white candy coating in a microwaveable bowl and heat in a microwave at 30 second intervals until they are completely melted.

6 Add 1–2 tablespoons of vegetable oil to thin the coating and stir well.

7 Dip 1 cm (1/2 in.) of the lollipop sticks into the candy coating and insert into the bottom of the dice pops. Leave to stand in the polystyrene block.

8 Dip the dice pops carefully into the melted candy until completely covered.

9 Carefully shake off any excess candy coating and place back in the polystyrene block until completely dry.

10 Ask an adult to cut out enough circles from black sugarpaste to assemble as the dots on the dice.

11 When completely dry, attach the dots to the dice pops with a small amount of edible glue.

1 Put all of the ingredients in a blender, reserving a few of the smaller berries for later. Ask an adult to process the mixture until smooth. (If you have not got a blender, place the ingredients into a bowl and ask an adult to blend the mixture with a hand-held electric whisk.)

2 Now add the reserved smaller berries to the mixture and pour into the lolly moulds. Place the moulds into a freezer.

3 When the mixture has partially frozen, rotate the moulds — this way the larger pieces of fruit won't clump together. Leave them to set for at least 4 hours, until solid.

4 Remove the lollies from the freezer and let them stand at room temperature for 5 minutes. Then, remove from the moulds and enjoy!

TOP TIP!
Double the ingredients and make lots of berry pops — great for when your friends come over!

MAKES 10-12

Extra equipment:
• blender
• ice lolly moulds

Ingredients:
• 225 g (8 oz) fresh mixed berries
• 50 g (2 oz) icing sugar
• 2 tablespoons clear honey
• 2 tablespoons lemon juice
• 900 ml (1 1/2 pt) natural yogurt

JELLY SUNDAE

1. Cut the lime jelly into cubes and put it into a heatproof jug. Ask an adult to prepare the jelly, following the packet instructions. Stir the jelly with a wooden spoon until it has all dissolved. Pour the jelly into one of the small dishes and place in the refrigerator to set.

2. Make the strawberry and orange jellies, as above.

3. Once the jelly has set, whip the cream until it forms stiff peaks.

4. Spoon a quarter of the lime jelly into each sundae glass. Then, spoon some whipped cream on top.

5. Next, spoon a quarter of the strawberry jelly in each glass, top with cream and then finally add the orange jelly.

6. Top with a small spoonful of whipped cream and sprinkle with chocolate strands to serve.

TOP TIP!
Decorate your jelly sundaes with fruit and mint leaves.

SERVES 4

Extra equipment:
- heatproof jug
- 3 small dishes
- whisk
- 4 sundae glasses

Ingredients:
- 135 g (5 oz) lime jelly
- 135 g (5 oz) strawberry jelly
- 135 g (5 oz) orange jelly
- 300 ml (10 fl.oz) double cream
- chocolate strands, to serve

1 Grease and line the baking tray.

2 Put the butter and golden syrup into a saucepan and melt over a gentle heat, stirring continuously, until well mixed.

3 Mix the oats, sugar, ground ginger, baking powder and ground nutmeg in a bowl.

4 Then, pour the butter mixture into the dry ingredients. Mix until well combined, then stir in the chopped stem ginger.

5 Pour the mixture into the baking tray and bake for 25–30 minutes, or until golden brown on top.

6 Remove the flapjacks from the oven and cool in the tin for 10 minutes. Then cut the flapjack into squares and put on a wire rack to cool completely.

TOP TIP!
Melt a little chocolate and drizzle over the flapjacks for an extra special treat.

MAKES 12

Extra equipment:
• 30 x 25.5 cm (12 x 10 in) baking tray
• baking paper

Ingredients:
• 225 g (8 oz) unsalted butter, plus extra for greasing
• 2 tablespoons golden syrup
• 450 g (1 lb) porridge oats
• 225 g (8 oz) soft light brown sugar
• 1 tablespoon ground ginger
• 1/2 teaspoon baking powder
• pinch ground nutmeg
• 1 piece stem ginger in syrup, finely chopped

Preheat the oven to 160°C / 140°C fan oven / 350°F / gas mark 4

INDEX OF RECIPES